Machines

priddy 😊 books
big ideas for little people

Monster truck

Monster trucks entertain crowds at shows by driving at high speed over old cars and crushing them. These trucks are enormous — their tyres alone are 1.6 metres high!

Standard pick-up truck body

Drag racer

These extremely powerful cars race in pairs along a straight track called a strip. Drag racers have huge engines that speed them along at up to 530 km/h. They are travelling so fast at the end of the strip that the driver has to release a parachute to help them slow down.

'Burning out' heats the tyres to give more grip

Stock car

Stock cars are regular cars which have been modified for racing. They are basic, stripped-down machines with an engine, chassis and suspension tuned to get maximum speed and power. Stock cars are raced around oval tracks at an average speed of 305 km/h.

Rear spoiler helps the car's road handling

Strengthened roll cage for driver safety

Rally cars are tuned-up versions of regular cars. They are raced in timed stages over roads, dirt tracks and through forests. The drivers skid, slide and jump these powerful cars around different circuits throughout the world in the fastest times possible.

Co-driver helps with directions

Four-wheel drive for extra control →

Rally car

Grand Prix cars are specially designed and built for racing. These very powerful, lightweight machines accelerate quickly, handle precisely and can reach speeds of around 370 km/h. Teams of drivers compete in a series of races in a year.

Rear spoiler keeps the car on the ground

Ultra-light body and chassis

Wide wheels for maximum grip

Grand Prix car

Superbike

Riders lean sharply when cornering

Protective clothing is essential

Superbike racing is one of the fastest
and most dangerous motorsports in the world.
The motorbikes are based on standard road machines, with
1,000-cc engines and only some minor modifications. On the
fastest circuits they can reach speeds of up to 314 km/h.

Dirt bike

Riders must wear helmets for protection

Dirt bikes are lightweight, powerful and accelerate very quickly. They are used in 'motocross', where riders race around dirt tracks. There are lots of steep bends and jumps, which make the machines fly high in the air!

Knobbly tyres for good grip

Strong suspension

Engine sizes range from 50 to 550 cc

Quad bikes, or ATVs (all-terrain vehicles) are four-wheeled machines designed for off-road riding. Standard quad bikes are popular on farms, while racing machines like this one are lighter and have stronger suspensions. In quad bike motocross, they race at speeds of more than 100 km/h.

Riders wear protective clothing

Engines up to 500 cc

Quad bike

Dune buggy

These vehicles are based on Volkswagen Beetle cars,
and are built to be driven on soft sand and beaches.
Also called 'sand rails', they are little more than a
steel frame with an engine and wheels attached!
They can reach up to 96 km/h and are great fun
to race and jump over big sand dunes.

Lightweight,
steel frame

Wide rear
tyres

Air-cooled
Volkswagen engine

Supercar

Driver sits in the middle, between two passenger seats

Very low, sporty design

The McLaren F1 is a classic supercar. Capable of reaching 386 km/h, it is one of the fastest road cars in the world and is also one of the most expensive! It is the closest thing to a Grand Prix race car that can be driven on the road.

Snowmobile

Snowmobiles, or 'skidoos' as they are also known, are fast machines built to drive across snow and ice. These vehicles can race at up to 110 km/h in 'snocross' racing events. Snowmobiles are also used for extreme sports, where the riders pull amazing stunts, flying high into the air.

Anti-glare visor helps with driving in snow

Steerable skis

Caterpillar track moves the snowmobile along

Fan drives the craft forward

'Skirt' fills with air

13

SACHA ROUCHIER

Hovercraft

Hovercraft are vehicles that can be driven on land or water. Their engines drive powerful fans that create a cushion of air for the craft to hover on, and be pushed forward by at the same time. There are larger crafts that carry vehicles and passengers, as well as small single-seaters that are raced at speeds of over 110 km/h.

Jumbo jet

Large passenger planes like this one are called jumbo jets. Flying at up to 909 km/h, each plane can carry up to 600 passengers. The best known jumbo jet is the Boeing 747.

Pilot and co-pilot fly the plane from the cockpit

The space shuttle is the world's only reusable spacecraft. When it is launched, the rocket engines burn more than 240,000 litres of fuel each minute. The two boosters detach after about two minutes and parachute to Earth. With a crew of seven astronauts, the shuttle orbits the earth at about 27,000 km/h.

Fuel tank, containing liquid oxygen and hydrogen

Rocket boosters detach at 45,000 metres

The main part of the shuttle is called the orbiter

USA

United States

NASA
Endeavour

Space shuttle

Airport fire truck

This extra-fast fire truck is used at airports. It has a special nozzle that can pierce through the body of an aircraft, pumping in water and foam to quickly put out a fire.

Extendable arm with special piercing nozzle

7615

3

This four-wheel drive crash rescue rig quickly responds to emergencies at airports and on highways. It carries chemicals, cutting tools and other specialist rescue equipment, along with a crew of five firefighters.

Emergency lights

CRASH FIRE RESCUE

OSHKOSH

R28

C497004

OSHKOSH

Rescue rig

Giant excavator

This huge excavating machine is used in quarries. It digs out massive amounts of rock and earth, which are used for building roads and houses. The caterpillar tracks, which move it across rough ground, are as tall as a man, and a small car would fit into the digging bucket!

Digging bucket, powered by hydraulics

RH75C

MM732

RH120C

MILLER

A bulldozer is a powerful machine used on building sites. Its 250-horsepower diesel engine moves it along on caterpillar tracks. Hydraulic pistons power the equipment that moves earth and rocks, levelling the ground for new roads or buildings.

Earth ripper breaks up very hard ground

The blade levels the ground

Bulldozer

Dump truck

The truck bed is loaded with earth and rocks

This huge dump truck can carry up to 200 tons of rocks and earth. It has a turbocharged, 1,000-horsepower engine and massive, 1.8-metre high wheels.

Huge wheels